Born in 1970

by

Kerry Butters.

Born in 1970.

Millennium: 2nd millennium

Centuries: 19th century – **20th century** – 21st century

Decades: 1940s 1950s 1960s – **1970s** – 1980s 1990s 2000s

Years: 1967 1968 1969 – **1970** – 1971 1972 1973

1970 (MCMLXX) was a common year starting on Thursday
(dominical letter D) of the Gregorian calendar, the 1970th year of
the Common Era (CE) and *Anno Domini* (AD) designations, the
970th year of the 2nd millennium, the 70th year of the
20th century, and the 1st year of the 1970s decade.

Contents

Events

January

- January 1 – Unix time begins at 00:00:00 UTC.
- January 4 – The 7.1 Mw Tonghai earthquake shakes Tonghai County, Yunnan province, China, with a maximum Mercalli intensity of X (*Extreme*). Between 10,000–15,621 were killed and 26,783 were injured.
- January 5 – The first episode of United States soap opera *All My Children* is broadcast on the ABC television network.
- January 12 – Biafra capitulates, ending the Nigerian Civil War.
- January 14 – Diana Ross and The Supremes perform their farewell live concert together at the Frontier Hotel in Las Vegas. Ross's replacement, Jean Terrell, is introduced onstage at the end of the last show.
- January 15 – After a 32-month fight for independence from Nigeria, Biafran forces under Philip Effiong formally surrender to General Yakubu Gowon.

- January 20 – The Greater London Council announces its plans for the Thames Barrier at Woolwich to prevent flooding (the barrier opens in 1981).
- January 21
  - Five lifeboatmen are killed when a Fraserburgh, Scotland vessel, *The Duchess of Kent*, capsizes.
  - Pan American Airways offers the first commercially scheduled 747 service from John F. Kennedy International Airport to London Heathrow Airport.
- January 23 – Joseph Fielding Smith becomes the 10th President of The Church of Jesus Christ of Latter-day Saints
- January 26 – Mick Jagger is fined £200 for possession of cannabis.

February

- February 1 – The Benavidez rail disaster near Buenos Aires, Argentina kills 236.
- February 10 – An avalanche at Val-d'Isère, France kills 39 tourists.
- February 11 – *Ōsumi*, Japan's first satellite, is launched on a Lambda-4 rocket.
- February 13 – Black Sabbath's eponymous debut album is released; often regarded as the first true heavy metal album.
- February 14 – The iconic live album *The Who: Live at Leeds* is recorded.
- February 17
  - MacDonald family massacre: Jeffrey R. MacDonald kills his wife and children at Fort Bragg, North Carolina, claiming that drugged-out "hippies" did it.

- February 11: Ōsumi (satellite) launched
- Author David Irving is ordered to pay £40,000 libel damages to Capt. John Broome over his book *The Destruction of Convoy PQ17*.
- February 18 – A jury finds the Chicago Seven defendants not guilty of conspiring to incite a riot, in charges stemming from the violence at the 1968 Democratic National Convention. Five of the defendants are found guilty on the lesser charge of crossing state lines to incite a riot.
- February 19 – Poseidon bubble: shares in Australian nickel mining company Poseidon NL, which stood at $0.80 in September 1969, peak at around $280 before the speculative bubble bursts.
- February 21 – Construction begins on the Boğaziçi Bridge crossing the Bosphorus in Istanbul.
- February 22 – Guyana becomes a Republic within the Commonwealth of Nations.
- February 26 – Chevrolet releases the second generation Camaro.

March

- March 1 – Rhodesia severs its last tie with the United Kingdom, declaring itself a republic.
- March 5 – The Nuclear Non-Proliferation Treaty goes into effect, after ratification by 56 nations.
- March 6
  - A bomb being constructed by members of the Weathermen and meant to be planted at a military

dance in New Jersey, explodes, killing 3 members of the organization.
- Süleyman Demirel of AP forms the new government of Turkey (32nd government).
- March 7
  - Citroën introduces the SM at the Geneva Auto Salon.
  - A solar eclipse passes along the Atlantic coast region. Totality is visible across southern Mexico and across the southeast coast of the United States, Nantucket, and Nova Scotia.
- March 12 – Teenagers in the United Kingdom vote for the first time, in a by-election in Bridgwater.
- March 15 – The Expo '70 World's Fair opens in Suita, Osaka, Japan.
- March 16 – The complete New English Bible is published.
- March 17 – My Lai Massacre: The United States Army charges 14 officers with suppressing information related to the incident.
- March 18
  - General Lon Nol ousts Prince Norodom Sihanouk of Cambodia.
  - United States Postal Service workers in New York City go on strike; the strike spreads to the state of California and the cities of Akron, Ohio, Philadelphia, Chicago, Boston, and Denver; 210,000 out of 750,000 U.S. postal employees walk out. President Nixon assigns military units to New York City post offices. The strike lasts 2 weeks.

- March 20 – The Agency for Cultural and Technical Co-operation (ACCT) (Agence de Coopération Culturelle et Technique) is founded.
- March 21
  - The first Earth Day proclamation is issued by San Francisco Mayor Joseph Alioto.
  - "All Kinds of Everything", sung by Dana (music and text by Derry Lindsay and Jackie Smith), wins the Eurovision Song Contest 1970 for Ireland.
- March 31
  - NASA's *Explorer 1*, the first American satellite and Explorer program spacecraft, reenters Earth's atmosphere after 12 years in orbit.
  - Japan Airlines Flight 351, carrying 131 passengers and 7 crew from Tokyo to Fukuoka, is hijacked by Japanese Red Army members. All passengers are eventually freed.

April 17: *Apollo 13* crew after splashdown.

April

- April 1
  - American President Richard Nixon signs the Public Health Cigarette Smoking Act into law, banning cigarette television advertisements in the United States from January 1, 1971.

- American Motors Corporation introduces the Gremlin.
- The 1970 United States Census begins. There are 203,392,031 United States residents on this day.
- April 4 – Fragments of burnt human remains believed to be those of Adolf Hitler, Eva Braun, Joseph Goebbels, Magda Goebbels and the Goebbels children are crushed and scattered in the Biederitz river at a KGB center in Magdeburg, East Germany.
- April 6 – BBC Radio 4 broadcasts the first edition of *PM*.
- April 8
  - A huge gas explosion at a subway construction site in Osaka, Japan kills 79 and injures over 400.
  - Israeli Air Force F-4 Phantom II fighter bombers kill 47 Egyptian school children at an elementary school in what is known as Bahr el-Baqar massacre. The single-floor school is hit by 5 bombs and 2 air-to-ground missiles.
- April 10
  - In a press release written in mock-interview style, that is included in promotional copies of his first solo album, Paul McCartney announces that he has left The Beatles.
  - The *Elton John* album is released, the second album by Elton John, but the first to chart and the first to be released in America.
- April 11
  - An avalanche at a tuberculosis sanatorium in the French Alps kills 74, mostly young boys.
  - Apollo program: *Apollo 13* (Jim Lovell, Fred Haise, Jack Swigert) is launched toward the Moon.

- April 13 – An oxygen tank in the Apollo 13 spacecraft explodes, forcing the crew to abort the mission and return in 4 days.

April 1: New car: AMC Gremlin

- April 16
    - Rev. Ian Paisley wins a by-election to gain a seat in the House of Commons of Northern Ireland.
    - The National Westminster Bank begins trading in the United Kingdom.
- April 17 – Apollo program: *Apollo 13* splashes down safely in the Pacific.
- April 21 – The Principality of Hutt River "secedes" from Australia (it remains unrecognised by Australia and other nations).
- April 22 – The first Earth Day is celebrated in the U.S.
- April 24 – China's first satellite (*Dong Fang Hong 1*) is launched into orbit using a Long March-1 Rocket (CZ-1).
- April 26 – The World Intellectual Property Organization (WIPO) is founded.
- April 29 – The U.S. invades Cambodia to hunt out the Viet Cong; widespread, large antiwar protests occur in the U.S.

May

- May 1 – Demonstrations against the trial of the New Haven Nine, Bobby Seale, and Ericka Huggins draw 12,000. President Richard Nixon orders U.S. forces to cross into neutral Cambodia, threatening to widen the Vietnam War, sparking nationwide riots and leading to the Kent State shootings.
- May 4 – Kent State shootings: Four students at Kent State University in Ohio are killed and 9 wounded by Ohio National Guardsmen, at a protest against the incursion into Cambodia.
- May 6
  - Arms Crisis in the Republic of Ireland: Charles Haughey and Neil Blaney are dismissed as members of the Irish Government, for accusations of their involvement in a plot to import arms for use by the Provisional IRA in Northern Ireland.
  - Feyenoord wins the European Cup after a 2–1 win over Celtic.
- May 8
  - Hard Hat Riot: Unionized construction workers attack about 1,000 students and others protesting the Kent State shootings near the intersection of Wall Street and Broad Street and at New York City Hall.
  - The Beatles release their 12th and final album, *Let It Be*.
  - The New York Knicks win their first NBA championship, defeating the Los Angeles Lakers 113-99 in Game 7 of the world championship series at Madison Square Garden.

- May 9 – In Washington, D.C., 100,000 people demonstrate against the Vietnam War.
- May 10 – The Boston Bruins win their first Stanley Cup since 1941 when Bobby Orr scores a goal 40 seconds into overtime for a 4-3 victory which completes a four-game sweep of the St. Louis Blues.
- May 11
  - Henry Marrow is killed in an alleged hate crime in Oxford, North Carolina.
  - Lubbock tornado: An F5 tornado hits downtown Lubbock, Texas, the first to hit a downtown district of a major city since Topeka, Kansas in 1966; 28 are killed.
- May 12 – The 1976 Winter Olympics are awarded to Denver, Colorado but it is later rejected in 1972.
- May 14
  - Ulrike Meinhof helps Andreas Baader escape and create the Red Army Faction which exists until 1998.
  - In the second day of violent demonstrations at Jackson State University in Jackson, Mississippi, state law enforcement officers fire into the demonstrators, killing 2 and injuring 12.
- May 17 – Thor Heyerdahl sets sail from Morocco on the papyrus boat *Ra II*, to sail the Atlantic Ocean.
- May 23 – A fire occurs in the Britannia Bridge over the Menai Strait near Bangor, Caernarfonshire, Wales, contributing to its partial destruction and amounting to approximately £1,000,000 worth of fire damage.
- May 24 – The scientific drilling of the Kola Superdeep Borehole begins in the USSR.

- May 26 – The Soviet Tupolev Tu-144 becomes the first commercial transport to exceed Mach 2.
- May 27 – A British expedition climbs the south face of Annapurna I.
- May 31
  - The 7.9 Mw Ancash earthquake shakes Peru with a maximum Mercalli intensity of VIII (*Severe*) and a landslide buries the town of Yungay, Peru. Between 66,794–70,000 were killed and 50,000 were injured.
  - The 1970 FIFA World Cup is inaugurated in Mexico.

June

- June 1 – *Soyuz 9*, a two-man spacecraft, is launched in the Soviet Union.
- June 2 – Norway announces it has rich oil deposits off its North Sea coast.
- June 4 – Tonga gains independence from the United Kingdom.
- June 7 – The Who become the first act to perform rock music (their rock opera, *Tommy*) at the Metropolitan Opera House, New York.
- June 8 – A coup in Argentina brings a new junta of service chiefs; on June 18, Roberto M. Levingston becomes President.
- June 11 – The United States gets its first female generals, Anna Mae Hays and Elizabeth P. Hoisington.
- June 12 – NDFLOAG guerrillas attack military garrisons at Izki and Nizwa in Oman.

- June 13 – The Long and Winding Road becomes the Beatles' 20th and final single to reach number one on the US Billboard Hot 100 chart.
- June 18 – United Kingdom general election, 1970: the Conservative Party wins and Edward Heath becomes Prime Minister, ousting the Labour government of Harold Wilson after nearly six years in power. The election result is something of a surprise, as most of the opinion polls had predicted a third successive Labour win.
- June 21
  - Brazil defeats Italy 4–1 to win the 1970 FIFA World Cup.
  - Penn Central declares Section 77 bankruptcy, the largest ever US corporate bankruptcy up to this date.
- June 24 – The United States Senate repeals the Gulf of Tonkin Resolution of 1964.
- June 28 – U.S. ground troops withdraw from Cambodia.
- June 30 – Riverfront Stadium in Cincinnati opens.

July

- July 1
  - Colorado State College changes its name to University of Northern Colorado.
  - The U.S. Food and Drug Administration (FDA) is subordinated to Public Health Service.
- July 3 – The French Army detonates a 914 kiloton thermonuclear device in the Mururoa Atoll. It is their fourth and largest nuclear test.
- July 4

- A chartered Dan-Air De Havilland Comet crashes into the mountains north of Barcelona; at least 112 people are killed.
- Bob Hope and other entertainers gather in Washington, D.C. for *Honor America Day*, a nonpartisan holiday event.
- Longtime radio music countdown show American Top 40 debuts on 5 U.S. stations with Casey Kasem as host.
- July 5 – Air Canada Flight 621 crashes at Toronto International Airport, Toronto, Ontario; all 109 passengers and crew are killed.
- July 11 – The first tunnel under the Pyrenees links the towns of Aragnouet (France) and Bielsa (Spain).
- July 12 – Thor Heyerdahl's papyrus boat *Ra II* arrives in Barbados.
- July 16 – Three Rivers Stadium in Pittsburgh opens.
- July 21 – The Aswan High Dam in Egypt is completed.
- July 23
  - Said bin Taimur, Sultan of Muscat and Oman, is deposed in a palace coup by his son, Qaboos.
  - Two CS gas canisters are thrown into the chamber of the British House of Commons.
- July 30 – Damages totalling £485,528 are awarded to 28 Thalidomide victims.
- July 31 – NBC anchor Chet Huntley retires from full-time broadcasting.

August

- August 7 – Harold Haley, Marin County Superior Court Judge, is taken hostage and murdered, in an effort to free George Jackson from police custody.
- August 17 –August 18 – The U.S. sinks 418 containers of nerve gas into the Gulf Stream near the Bahamas.
- August 17 – Venera program: *Venera 7* is launched toward Venus. It later becomes the first spacecraft to successfully transmit data from the surface of another planet.
- August 26 – Women's Strike for Equality takes place down Fifth Avenue in New York City.
- August 26 –August 30 – The Isle of Wight Festival 1970 takes place on East Afton Farm off the coast of England. Some 600,000 people attend the largest rock festival of all time. Artists include Jimi Hendrix, The Who, The Doors, Chicago, Richie Havens, John Sebastian, Joan Baez, Ten Years After, Emerson, Lake & Palmer, The Moody Blues and Jethro Tull.
- August 29 – Rubén Salazar is shot and killed during a rally in East Los Angeles.

September

- September 1 – An assassination attempt against King Hussein of Jordan precipitates the Black September crisis.
- September 3 – September 6 – Israeli forces fight Palestinian guerillas in southern Lebanon.
- September 5
  - Vietnam War – Operation Jefferson Glenn: The United States 101st Airborne Division and the South

Vietnamese 1st Infantry Division initiate a new operation in Thua Thien Province (the operation ends in October 1971).

- Formula One driver Jochen Rindt is killed in qualifying for the Italian *Grand Prix*. He becomes World Driving Champion anyhow, first to earn the honor posthumously.

- September 6 – Dawson's Field hijackings, The Popular Front for the Liberation of Palestine hijacks 4 passenger aircraft from Pan Am, TWA and Swissair on flights to New York from Brussels, Frankfurt and Zürich.
- September 7
  - An anti-war rally is held at Valley Forge, Pennsylvania, attended by John Kerry, Jane Fonda and Donald Sutherland.
  - Fighting breaks out between Arab guerillas and government forces in Amman, Jordan.
- September 8 –September 10 – The Jordanian government and Palestinian guerillas make repeated unsuccessful truces.
- September 9
  - Guinea recognizes East Germany.
  - Elvis Presley begins his first concert tour since 1958 in Phoenix, Arizona, at the Veterans Memorial Coliseum.
- September 10
  - Cambodian government forces break the siege of Kompong Tho after 3 months.
  - The Chevrolet Vega is introduced.
- September 11 – The Ford Pinto is introduced.
- September 13

- The covert incursion of Operation Tailwind is instigated by the American forces in southeast Laos.
- The first New York City Marathon begins.
- September 15 – King Hussein of Jordan forms a military government with Muhammad Daoud as the prime minister.
- September 18 – American musician Jimi Hendrix dies from an overdose of sleeping pills.
- September 20
  - Syrian armored forces cross the Jordanian border.
  - *Luna 16* lands on the Moon and lifts off the next day with samples. It lands on Earth September 24.
- September 21
  - Palestinian armored forces reinforce Palestinian guerillas in Irbidi, Jordan.
  - *Monday Night Football* debuts on ABC; the Cleveland Browns defeat the New York Jets 31-21 in front of more than 85,000 fans at Cleveland Stadium.
- September 22
  - The International Hydrographic Organization (IHO) is founded.
  - Tunku Abdul Rahman resigns as prime minister of Malaysia, and is succeeded by his deputy Tun Abdul Razak.
- September 23 – The first women's only tennis tournament begins in Houston, known as the Houston Women's Invitation.
- September 26 – The Laguna Fire starts in San Diego County, burning 175,425 acres (709.92 km^2).

- September 27 – Richard Nixon begins a tour of Europe, visiting Italy, Yugoslavia, Spain, the United Kingdom and Ireland.
- September 28 – Gamal Abdel Nasser dies; Vice President Anwar Sadat is named temporary president of Egypt.
- September 29
  - The U.S. Congress gives President Richard Nixon authority to sell arms to Israel.
  - In Berlin, Baader-Meinhof Gang members rob 3 banks, with loot totaling over DM200,000.

October

- October 2
  - Under the National Environmental Policy Act (NEPA) the Environmental Science Services Administration (ESSA) Corps, one of seven federal uniformed services of the United States, is renamed to NOAA Commissioned Officer Corps under the soon to be formed National Oceanic and Atmospheric Administration (NOAA).
  - The Wichita State University football team's "Gold" plane crashes in Colorado, killing most of the players. They were on their way (along with administrators and fans) to a game with Utah State University.
  - Pink Floyd releases *Atom Heart Mother*. It becomes their first number 1 album.
- October 3
  - In Lebanon, the government of Prime Minister Rashid Karami resigns.

- o The National Oceanic and Atmospheric Administration (NOAA) is formed.
- o The Weather Bureau is renamed to National Weather Service, as part of NOAA.
- October 4
  - o Jochen Rindt becomes Formula One World Driving Champion, first to earn the honor posthumously.
  - o In Bolivia, Army Commander General Rogelio Miranda and a group of officers rebel and demand the resignation of President Alfredo Ovando Candía, who fires him.
  - o National Educational Television ends operations, being succeeded by PBS.
- October 5
  - o U.S. President Richard Nixon's European tour ends.
  - o The Front de libération du Québec (FLQ) kidnaps James Cross in Montreal and demands release of all its imprisoned members. The next day the Canadian government announces it will not meet the demand, beginning Quebec's October Crisis.
  - o The Public Broadcasting Service begins broadcasting.
- October 6
  - o Bolivian President Alfredo Ovando Candía resigns; General Rogelio Miranda takes over but resigns soon after.
  - o French President Georges Pompidou visits the Soviet Union.
- October 7 – General Juan José Torres becomes the new President of Bolivia.
- October 8

- The U.S. Foreign Office announces that renewal of arms sales to Pakistan.
- Soviet author Aleksandr Solzhenitsyn is awarded the Nobel Prize in Literature.
- Vietnam War: In Paris, a Communist delegation rejects U.S. President Richard Nixon's October 7 peace proposal as "a maneuver to deceive world opinion."
- October 9 – The Khmer Republic is proclaimed in Cambodia which begins the Civil War with the Khmer Rouge.
- October 10
  - Fiji becomes independent.
  - October Crisis: In Montreal, a national crisis hits Canada when Quebec Minister of Labour Pierre Laporte becomes the second statesman kidnapped by members of the FLQ terrorist group.
- October 11 – Eleven French soldiers are killed in a shootout with rebels in Chad.
- October 12 – Vietnam War: U.S. President Richard Nixon announces that the United States will withdraw 40,000 more troops before Christmas.
- October 13
  - Canada and the People's Republic of China establish diplomatic relations.
  - Saeb Salam forms a government in Lebanon.
- October 14 – A Chinese nuclear test is conducted in Lop Nor.
- October 15
  - In Egypt, a referendum supports Anwar Sadat 90.04%.
  - A section of the new West Gate Bridge in Melbourne collapses into the river below, killing 35 construction workers.

- The domestic Soviet Aeroflot Flight 244 is hijacked and diverted to Turkey.
- October 16 – October Crisis: The Canadian government declares a state of emergency and outlaws the Quebec Liberation Front.
- October 17
  - October Crisis: Pierre Laporte is found murdered in south Montreal.
  - A cholera epidemic breaks out in Istanbul.
  - Anwar Sadat officially becomes President of Egypt.
- October 20
  - The Soviet Union launches the *Zond 8* lunar probe.
  - Egyptian president Anwar Sadat names Mahmoud Fawzi as his prime minister.
- October 21 – A U.S. Air Force plane makes an emergency landing near Leninakan, Soviet Union. The Soviets release the American officers, including 2 generals, November 10.
- October 22 – Chilean army commander René Schneider is shot in Santiago; the government declares a state of emergency. Schneider dies October 25.
- October 24 – Salvador Allende is elected President of Chile.
- October 25 – The wreck of the Confederate submarine *Hunley* is found off Charleston, South Carolina, by pioneer underwater archaeologist, Dr. E. Lee Spence, then just 22 years old. *Hunley* was the first submarine in history to sink a ship in warfare.
- October 26 – Garry Trudeau's comic strip *Doonesbury* debuts in approximately two dozen newspapers in the United States.
- October 28

- In Jordan, the government of Ahmed Toukan resigns; the next prime minister is Wasfi al-Tal.
- A cholera outbreak in eastern Slovakia causes Hungary to close its border with Czechoslovakia.
- Gary Gabelich drives the rocket-powered *Blue Flame* to an official land speed record at 622.407 mph (1,001.667 km/h) on the dry lake bed of the Bonneville Salt Flats in Utah. The record, the first above 1 000 km/h, stands for nearly 13 years.

- October 30 – In Vietnam, the worst monsoon to hit the area in 6 years causes large floods, kills 293, leaves 200,000 homeless and virtually halts the Vietnam War.

November

- November 1 – Club Cinq-Sept fire in Saint-Laurent-du-Pont, France, kills 146.
- (November 1) polish vice president killed at Karachi airport, Pakistan
- November 3
  - Democrats sweep the U.S. Congressional midterm elections; Ronald Reagan is reelected governor of California; Jimmy Carter is elected governor of Georgia.
  - Salvador Allende becomes president of Chile.
- November 4
  - Vietnam War – Vietnamization: The United States turns control of the air base in the Mekong Delta to South Vietnam.

- Social workers in Los Angeles take custody of Genie, a girl who had been kept in solitary confinement since her birth.
- November 5 – Vietnam War: The United States Military Assistance Command in Vietnam reports the lowest weekly American soldier death toll in 5 years (24 soldiers die that week, which is the fifth consecutive week the death toll is below 50; 431 are reported wounded that week, however).
- November 8
  - Egypt, Libya and Sudan announce their intentions to form a federation.
  - Tom Dempsey, who was born with a deformed right foot and right hand, sets a National Football League record by kicking a 63-yard field goal to lift the New Orleans Saints to a 19-17 victory over the Detroit Lions at Tulane Stadium.
  - The British comedy television series, *The Goodies* debuts on BBC 2.
- November 9
  - The Soviet Union launches *Luna 17*.
  - Vietnam War: The Supreme Court of the United States votes 6–3 not to hear a case by the state of Massachusetts, about the constitutionality of a state law granting Massachusetts residents the right to refuse military service in an undeclared war.
- November 10 – Vietnam War – Vietnamization: For the first time in 5 years, an entire week ends with no reports of United States combat fatalities in Southeast Asia.
- November 12 – Soviet author Andrei Amalrik is sentenced to 3 years for 'anti-Soviet' writings.

- November 13
    - Hafez al-Assad comes to power in Syria, following a military coup within the Ba'ath Party.
    - 1970 Bhola cyclone: A 120-mph (193 km/h) tropical cyclone hits the densely populated Ganges Delta region of East Pakistan (now Bangladesh), killing an estimated 500,000 people (considered the 20th century's worst cyclone disaster). It gives rise to the temporary island of New Moore / South Talpatti.
- November 14
    - Southern Airways Flight 932 crashes in Wayne County, West Virginia; all 75 on board, including 37 players and 5 coaches from the Marshall University football team, are killed.
    - The Soviet Union enters the ICAO, making Russian the fourth official language of the organization.
- November 16 – The Lockheed L-1011 TriStar flies for the first time.
- November 17
    - Vietnam War: Lieutenant William Calley goes on trial for the My Lai Massacre.
    - Luna programme: The Soviet Union lands *Lunokhod 1* on Mare Imbrium (Sea of Rains) on the Moon. This is the first roving remote-controlled robot to land on another world, and is released by the orbiting Luna 17 spacecraft.
- November 18
    - U.S. President Richard Nixon asks the U.S. Congress for US$155 million in supplemental aid for the Cambodian government (US $85 million is for military assistance to

prevent the overthrow of the government of Premier
Lon Nol by the Khmer Rouge and North Vietnam).

- o The United Nations Security Council demands that no
  government recognize Rhodesia.
- November 19 – European Economic Community prime
  ministers meet in Munich.
- November 21
  - o Syrian Prime Minister Hafez al-Assad forms a new
    government but retains the post of defense minister.
  - o In Ethiopia, the Eritrean Liberation Front kills an
    Ethiopian general.
  - o Vietnam War – Operation Ivory Coast: A joint Air Force
    and Army team raids the Sơn Tây prison camp in an
    attempt to free American POWs thought to be held
    there (no Americans are killed, but the prisoners have
    already moved to another camp; all U.S. POWs are
    moved to a handful of central prison complexes as a
    result of this raid).
- November 22 – Guinean president Ahmed Sékou Touré
  accuses Portugal of an attack when hundreds of mercenaries
  land near the capital Conakry.
- November 23–24 – The Guinean army repels the landing
  attempts.
- November 23 – Rodgers and Hammerstein's *Oklahoma!*
  makes its network TV debut, when CBS telecasts the 1955
  film version as a 3-hour Thanksgiving special.
- November 25–November 29 – A U.N. delegation arrives to
  investigate the Guinea situation.
- November 25 – In Tokyo, author and Tatenokai militia
  leader Yukio Mishima and his followers take over the

headquarters of the Japan Self-Defense Forces in an attempted coup d'état. After Mishima's speech fails to sway public opinion towards his right-wing political beliefs, including restoration of the powers of the Emperor, he commits seppuku (public ritual suicide).

- November 26
  - East Pakistan leader Sheikh Mujibur Rahman accuses the central government of negligence in catastrophe relief.
  - Pope Paul VI begins an Asian tour.
- November 27 – Bolivian artist Benjamin Mendoza tries to assassinate Pope Paul VI during his visit in Manila.
- November 28 – The Montréal Alouettes defeated the Calgary Stampeders to become victors in the 58th Grey Cup 23-10.
- November 30 – British Caledonian Airways Ltd. (BCal) is formed.

December

- December 1
  - The Italian House of Representatives accepts the new divorce law.
  - Ethiopia recognizes the People's Republic of China.
  - The Basque ETA kidnaps West German Eugen Beihl in San Sebastián.
  - Luis Echeverría becomes president of Mexico.
- December 2 – The United States Environmental Protection Agency is established.
- December 3 – October Crisis: In Montreal, kidnapped British Trade Commissioner James Cross is released by the Front de

libération du Québec terrorist group after being held hostage for 60 days. Police negotiate his release and in return the Government of Canada grants 5 terrorists from the FLQ's Chenier Cell their request for safe passage to Cuba.

- December 3 – Burgos Trial: In Burgos, Spain, the trial of 16 Basque terrorism suspects begins.
- December 4
    - The Spanish government declares a 3-month martial law in the Basque county of Guipuzco, over strikes and demonstrations.
    - The U.N. announces that Portuguese navy and army units were responsible for the attempted invasion of Guinea.
- December 5
    - The Asian and Australian tour of Pope Paul VI ends.
    - Fluminense wins the Brazil Football Championship.
- December 7
    - Giovanni Enrico Bucher, the Swiss ambassador to Brazil, is kidnapped in Rio de Janeiro; kidnappers demand the release of 70 political prisoners.
    - The U.N. General Assembly supports the isolation of South Africa for its apartheid policies.
    - During his visit to the Polish capital, German Chancellor Willy Brandt goes down on his knees in front of a monument to the victims of the Warsaw Ghetto, which will become known as the Warschauer Kniefall ("Warsaw Genuflection").
- December 12 – A landslide in western Colombia leaves 200 dead.

- December 13 – The government of Poland announces food price increases. Riots and looting lead to a bloody confrontation between the rioters and the government on December 15.
- December 15
  - The USSR's *Venera 7* becomes the first spacecraft to land successfully on Venus and transmit data back to Earth.
  - The South Korean ferry *Namyong Ho* capsizes off Korea Strait; 308 people are killed.
- December 16 – The Ethiopian government declares a state of emergency in the county of Eritrea over the activities of the Eritrean Liberation Front.
- December 17 – Polish 1970 protests: Soldiers fire on civilians returning to work in Gdynia. Martial law is imposed in the country until December 22.
- December 20
  - General Secretary of the Polish United Workers' Party, Władysław Gomułka, resigns; Edward Gierek replaces him.
  - An Egyptian delegation leaves for Moscow to ask for economic and military aid.
- December 21 – The Grumman F-14 Tomcat makes its first flight.
- December 22
  - The Libyan Revolutionary Council declares that it will nationalize all foreign banks in the country.
  - Franz Stangl, the ex-commander of Treblinka, is sentenced to life imprisonment.
- December 23
  - The Polish government freezes food prices for 2 years.

- The Bolivian government releases Régis Debray.
- The North Tower of the World Trade Center is topped out at 1,368 feet (417 m), making it the tallest building in the world.
- Law 70-001 is enacted in the Democratic Republic of the Congo, amending article 4 of the constitution and making the country a one-party state.
- December 25 – The ETA releases Eugen Beihl.
- December 27 – India's president declares new elections.
- December 28
  - Burgos Trial: Three Basques are sentenced to death, twelve others sentenced to imprisonment (terms from 12 to 62 years), and one is released.
  - The suspected killers of Pierre Laporte, Jacques and Paul Rose and Francis Sunard, are arrested near Montreal.
- December 29 – U.S. President Richard Nixon signs into law the Occupational Safety and Health Act.
- December 30 – In Viscaya in the Basque country of Spain, 15,000 go on strike in protest at the Burgos trial death sentences. Francisco Franco commutes the sentences to 30 years in prison.
- December 31 – Paul McCartney sues in Britain to dissolve The Beatles' legal partnership.

Date unknown

- The Roman Catholic Church creates the first female Doctors of the Church, Saints Catherine of Siena and Teresa of Ávila.
- The first Regional Technical Colleges open in Ireland.
- Sada Abe, Japanese former prostitute and later actress, disappears.
- The Sweet Track is discovered in England. It was the world's oldest engineered roadway at the time of its discovery.
- Alvin Toffler publishes his book *Future Shock*.
- Sammlung zeitgenössischer Kunst der Bundesrepublik Deutschland, the Federal collection of contemporary art, is established in Germany.
- Xerox PARC computer laboratory opens in Palo Alto, California.
- The American Football League and NFL merge, creating the National Football Conference and American Football Conference. All AFL teams go to the AFC with a few NFL teams while the NFC is composed entirely of NFL teams.

Births

January

Lara Fabian

Skeet Ulrich

Minnie Driver

- January 2
  - Royce Clayton, American baseball player
  - Eric Whitacre, American composer
- January 3 – Christian Duguay, American comic actor
- January 4 – Chris Kanyon, American professional wrestler (d. 2010)
- January 6
  - Julie Chen, American television news anchor and host
  - Keenan McCardell, American football player
  - Gabrielle Reece, American volleyball player and model
- January 7
  - Todd Day, American basketball player
  - Doug E. Doug, American comedian, actor and director
- January 9 – Lara Fabian, Canadian/Belgian singer
- January 12 – Zack de la Rocha, American musician
- January 13
  - Marco Pantani, Italian cyclist (d. 2004)
  - Shonda Rhimes, American television producer and writer
- January 15 – Shane McMahon, American professional wrestler and wrestling executive
- January 17
  - Jeremy Roenick, American hockey player
  - Genndy Tartakovsky, Russian animator
- January 18 – DJ Quik, American rapper and producer
- January 19
  - Tim Foster, British rower
  - Udo Suzuki, Japanese comedian
- January 20 – Skeet Ulrich, American actor
- January 22 – Alex Ross, American comic artist

- January 24 – Matthew Lillard, American actor
- January 27 – Adam Brand, Australian singer
- January 29
    - Heather Graham, American actress
    - Rajyavardhan Singh Rathore, Indian shooter
    - Paul Ryan, an American politician from the Republican Party, Mitt Romney's running mate in the 2012 United States presidential election
- January 31 – Minnie Driver, English actress

February

Simon Pegg

- February 1 – Malik Sealy, American basketball player (d. 2000)
- February 3
    - Keith Carney, American hockey player
    - Warwick Davis, English actor
- February 8
    - Stephanie Courtney, American actress and comedian
    - John Filan, Australian footballer
    - Alonzo Mourning, American basketball player
- February 9 – Glenn McGrath, Australian test cricketer
- February 10

- o Sarah Aldrich, American actress
- o Myrea Pettit, English fantasy & fairy artist and illustrator
- o Ardy Wiranata, Indonesian badminton player
- February 11 – Fredrik Thordendal, Swedish musician
- February 14
  - o Sean Hill, American hockey player
  - o Simon Pegg, British comedian, actor and writer
- February 16 – Armand Van Helden, American DJ and music producer
- February 17
  - o Tommy Moe, American Alpine skier
  - o Dominic Purcell, English-Australian actor
- February 18 – Raine Maida, Canadian musician and beat poet
- February 21 – Dayna Devon, American news anchor
- February 22 – Dominic Roussel, Canadian ice hockey player
- February 24 – Jeff Garcia, American football player
- February 26
  - o Linda Brava, Finnish violinist
  - o Cathrine Lindahl, Swedish curler
- February 27 – Matthias Lechner, German art director
- February 28
  - o Daniel Handler, American author
  - o Noureddine Morceli, Algerian athlete

March

Julie Bowen

Rachel Weisz

Queen Latifah

Vince Vaughn

- March 2 – Alexander Armstrong, English comedian, actor and presenter
- March 3 – Julie Bowen, American actress
- March 5
  - John Frusciante, American rock musician
  - Lisa Robin Kelly, American actress (d. 2013)
- March 7
  - Vladislav Adelkhanov, Russian classical violinist and writer
  - Jeff Hordley, English actor (*Emmerdale*)
  - Rachel Weisz, British-American actress
- March 8 – Jason Elam, American football player
- March 9 – Martin Johnson, English rugby player
- March 10
  - Michel van der Aa, Dutch composer
  - Antonio Edwards, American football player
- March 11 – Jane Slavin, British actress and author
- March 12 – Dave Eggers, American memoirist, writer and publisher
- March 16 – Paul Oscar (Páll Óskar Hjálmtýsson), Icelandic pop singer, songwriter and disc jockey

- March 18 – Queen Latifah, African-American rapper, record producer, and actress
- March 20
  - Michele Jaffe, American novelist
  - Michael Rapaport, American actor
  - Bernhard Hoëcker, German comedian
- March 21 – Shiho Niiyama, Japanese voice actress (d. 2000)
- March 22 – Leontien van Moorsel, Dutch cyclist
- March 24
  - Lara Flynn Boyle, American actress
  - Sharon Corr, Irish musician (The Corrs)
- March 27
  - Elizabeth Mitchell, American actress
  - Leila Pahlavi, Iranian princess (d. 2001)
- March 28 – Vince Vaughn, American actor, writer, and producer
- March 30 – Alenka Bratušek, Prime Minister of Slovenia

April

Jason Lee

Uma Thurman

Nicklas Lidstrom

- April 4
  - Sean Kelly, Canadian musician
  - Barry Pepper, Canadian actor
- April 5 – Miho Hatori, Japanese singer and songwriter
- April 10 – Q-Tip, American musician and actor
- April 11 – Trevor Linden, Canadian hockey player
- April 12 – Nick Hexum, American musician, 311 (band)
- April 13
  - Eduardo Capetillo, Mexican actor and singer
  - Ricky Schroder, American actor
- April 15 – Flex Alexander, American actor

- April 17 – Redman, American rapper, record producer, and actor
- April 18 – Heike Friedrich, German swimmer
- April 19 – Luis Miguel, Mexican singer
- April 20 – Adriano Moraes, Brazilian rodeo performer
- April 21 – Nicole Sullivan, American actress, comedian, and writer
- April 22 – Regine Velasquez, Filipino singer, actress, model and record producer
- April 23
  - Sadao Abe, Japanese actor
  - Andrew Gee, Australian rugby league footballer
  - Hans Välimäki, Finnish cook
- April 25
  - Tomoko Kawakami, Japanese voice actress (d. 2011)
  - Jason Lee, American skateboarder and actor
- April 26 – Tionne Watkins, American actress, and singer-songwriter from (TLC)
- April 28
  - Diego Simeone, Argentine footballer and manager
  - Nicklas Lidström, Swedish former hockey player
- April 29
  - Andre Agassi, American tennis player
  - Uma Thurman, American actress
- April 30 – Halit Ergenç, Turkish actor

May

Will Arnett

Tina Fey

Matt Flynn

Naomi Campbell

Joseph Fiennes

- May 3 – Jeffrey Sebelia, American fashion designer
- May 4
  - Will Arnett, Canadian actor
  - Karla Homolka, Canadian serial killer and rapist
- May 5
  - Kyan Douglas, Television personality
  - Todd Newton, American television personality
- May 6
  - Roland Kun, Nauruan politician
  - Kavan Smith, Canadian actor
- May 8
  - Michael Bevan, Australian cricketer
  - Luis Enrique, Spanish footballer
  - Naomi Klein, American cultural critic
- May 9 – Doug Christie, NBA basketball player and TV personality
- May 10 – Angelica Agurbash, Belarusian singer and former model
- May 12
  - Eric Champion, American Christian musician
  - Samantha Mathis, American actress

- May 15
    - Ronald and Frank de Boer, Dutch footballers
    - Rod Smith, American football player
- May 16 – Gabriela Sabatini, Argentine tennis player
- May 17 – Jordan Knight, American singer (*New Kids on the Block*)
- May 18 – Tina Fey, American writer, comedian, and actress
- May 19
    - K.J. Choi, South Korean golfer
    - Mario Dumont, Canadian politician
    - Jason Gray-Stanford, Canadian actor
- May 20 – Juliana Pasha, Albanian singer
- May 22 – Naomi Campbell, British model and actress
- May 23
    - Matt Flynn, American musician (Maroon 5)
    - Robert Peirce, American attorney
- May 24 – Jeff Zgonina, American football player
- May 25
    - Jamie Kennedy, American actor and comedian
    - Octavia Spencer, African-American actress
    - Satsuki Yukino, Japanese voice actress
- May 26 – Nobuhiro Watsuki, Japanese cartoonist
- May 27 – Joseph Fiennes, English actor
- May 30 – Jeffrey Sebelia, American fashion designer

June

Paul Thomas Anderson

Chris O'Donnell

- June 1 – Alexi Lalas, American soccer player
- June 3
  - Ammon McNeely, American rock climber
  - Peter Tägtgren, Swedish musician
- June 4
  - Deborah Compagnoni, Italian alpine skier
  - Izabella Scorupco, Polish model and actress
- June 6
  - Andrian Dushev, Bulgarian canoeist
  - Anthony Norris, American professional wrestler
- June 7
  - Ronaldo da Costa, Brazilian long-distance runner

- o Mike Modano, American hockey player
- June 8
  - o Gabrielle Giffords, American politician
  - o Kelli Williams, American actress
- June 10 – Katsuhiro Harada, Japanese game designer, director and producer at Bandai Namco Entertainment
- June 13
  - o Rivers Cuomo, American musician
  - o Mikael Ljungberg, Swedish wrestler (d. 2004)
- June 15
  - o Claus Norreen, Danish musician and record producer (Aqua)
  - o Leah Remini, American actress
- June 16
  - o Younus AlGohar, spiritualist, author, poet, Sufi, and humanitarian
  - o Phil Mickelson, American golfer
- June 17
  - o Will Forte, American writer, actor and comedian
  - o Sasha Sokol, Mexican singer
  - o Michael Showalter, American actor, comedian, writer, & director
- June 18 – Katie Derham, British newsreader
- June 19 – Quincy Watts, American athlete
- June 20
  - o Russell Garcia, British field hockey player
  - o Moulay Rachid, Prince of Morocco
  - o Michelle Reis, Hong Kong actress and beauty queen
  - o Athol Williams, South African poet and social philosopher

- June 21 – Pete Rock, American rapper/DJ/producer
- June 22
  - Michel Elefteriades, Greek-Lebanese politician, artist, producer and businessman
  - Freddy Soto, American comedian and actor
- June 24 – Glenn Medeiros, American singer and songwriter
- June 25
  - Lucy Benjamin, British actress
  - Roope Latvala, Finnish guitarist (Children of Bodom)
- June 26
  - Paul Thomas Anderson, American screenwriter and director
  - Sean Hayes, American actor
  - Patrick Norton, American writer and television host
  - Chris O'Donnell, American actor
  - Nick Offerman, American actor, writer and carpenter
- June 27
  - Jim Edmonds, American baseball player
  - Jo Frost, English nanny and television host
- June 28 – Steve Burton, American actor

July

Teemu Selänne

Beck

Christopher Nolan

- July 2 – Steve Morrow, Northern Irish footballer
- July 3
    - Teemu Selänne, National Hockey League player
    - Shawnee Smith, American actress
- July 5 – Mac Dre, American rapper (d. 2004)
- July 7 – Wayne McCullough, Northern Irish boxer
- July 8 – Beck, American singer
- July 9 – Trent Green, National Football League quarterback
- July 10
    - Jason Orange, British singer (Take That)
    - John Simm, British actor
- July 11
    - Justin Chambers, American actor and fashion model
    - Saj Karim, British politician
- July 19 – Nicola Sturgeon, Scottish politician
- July 23 – Thea Dorn, German writer

- July 25 – Julien Fountain, English Cricket Coach
- July 29 – Andi Peters, British TV presenter and producer
- July 30 – Christopher Nolan, English screenwriter and director

August

Kevin Smith

M. Night Shyamalan

Claudia Schiffer

Queen Rania of Jordan

Melissa McCarthy

- August 1
  - Quentin Coryatt, American football player
  - David James, English football goalkeeper
- August 2
  - Tony Amonte, American hockey player
  - Kevin Smith, American screenwriter, film director, and actor
- August 3 – Masahiro Sakurai, Japanese video game director, designer and writer
- August 4 – Pete Abrams, American webcomic artist
- August 5 – James Gunn, American filmmaker
- August 6 – M. Night Shyamalan, Indian-American film director, writer, producer, and actor
- August 9 – Thomas Lennon, American actor, comedian, and writer

- August 10
  - Bret Hedican, American ice hockey player
  - Brendon Julian, New Zealanders Cricket player
  - Steve Mautone, Australian Football player and coach
- August 12 – Jim Schlossnagle, American baseball coach
- August 13
  - Will Clarke, American novelist
  - Alan Shearer, English footballer
- August 14 – Leah Purcell, Australian actress
- August 16
  - Bonnie Bernstein, American sportscaster
  - Dean Del Mastro, Canadian politician
  - Saif Ali Khan, Indian actor
  - Manisha Koirala, Indian actress
- August 17 – Jim Courier, American tennis player
- August 18 – Malcolm-Jamal Warner, African-American actor
- August 20
  - John D. Carmack, American computer game programmer
  - Fred Durst, American rapper (Limp Bizkit)
- August 21 – Erik Dekker, Dutch professional cyclist
- August 22 – Ricco Groß, German biathlete
- August 23
  - Jay Mohr, American actor and comedian
  - River Phoenix, American actor (d. 1993)
  - Fabian Wilnis, Dutch footballer
- August 25 – Claudia Schiffer, German model
- August 26
  - Olimpiada Ivanova, Russian race walker
  - Melissa McCarthy, American actress and comedian

- August 27
  - Peter Ebdon, English snooker player
  - Jim Thome, American baseball player
- August 28 – Sherrié Austin, Australian actress and singer
- August 29 – Jacco Eltingh, Dutch tennis player
- August 30 – Guang Liang, Malaysian singer
- August 31
  - Debbie Gibson, American singer
  - Epic Mazur, American singer and rapper (Crazy Town)
  - Queen Rania of Jordan, Queen consort of Jordan
  - Zack Ward, Canadian actor

September

Taraji P. Henson

- September 1 – Hwang Jung-min, South Korean actor
- September 4
  - Daisy Dee, Dutch singer and actress
  - Ione Skye, British-born American actress
- September 5 – Liam Lynch, American musician, comedian, and puppetteer
- September 7

- o Gao Min, Chinese diver
- o Tom Everett Scott, American actor
- September 8
  - o Benny Ibarra, Mexican singer
  - o Latrell Sprewell, American basketball player
- September 10
  - o Molly McKay, LGBT activist
  - o Ménélik, French rapper
- September 11
  - o Taraji P. Henson, African-American actress
  - o Laura Wright, American actress
- September 13 – Susumu Chiba, Japanese voice actor
- September 14
  - o Mike Burns (soccer), American soccer player
- September 15 – Jukka Jokikokko, Finnish musician and studio engineer
- September 18 – Darren Gough, English cricketer
- September 19
  - o Dan Bylsma, American ice hockey player
  - o Yuka Imai, Japanese voice actress
  - o Takanori Nishikawa, Japanese singer
- September 20 – Gert Verheyen, Belgian footballer
- September 21 – Samantha Power, Irish-American academic, government official, Pulitzer Prize–winning writer
- September 22
  - o Mike Matheny, American baseball player
  - o Mystikal, African-American rapper
- September 23 – Ani DiFranco, American musician
- September 25 – Aja Kong, Japanese professional wrestler
- September 26

- Marco Etcheverry, Bolivian football player
- Frank Guinta, Mayor of Manchester, New Hampshire
- Yukio Iketani, Japanese gymnast
- September 27 – Yoshiharu Habu, Japanese professional shogi player
- September 28
  - Isabelle Brasseur, Canadian figure skater
  - Kimiko Date-Krumm, Japanese tennis player
- September 29
  - Joe Doucet, American designer, inventor and artist
  - Emily Lloyd, English actress
  - Yoshihiro Tajiri, Japanese professional wrestler
  - Natasha Gregson Wagner, American actress
- September 30 – Mark Smith, former *Gladiator*

October

Kelly Ripa

Matt Damon

Kirk Cameron

- October 1 – Moses Kiptanui, Kenyan athlete
- October 2 – Kelly Ripa, American actress and talk-show hostess
- October 4
  - Richard Hancox, English footballer
  - Zdravko Zdravkov, Bulgarian footballer
- October 8
  - Matt Damon, American actor
  - Tetsuya Nomura, Japanese video game and film director
- October 9 – Annika Sörenstam, Swedish golfer
- October 10
  - Silke Kraushaar, German luger
  - Sir Matthew Pinsent, British Olympic winning rower

- October 11
  - Lee Bong-Ju, South Korean long-distance runner
  - Andy Marriott, English footballer
- October 12
  - Kirk Cameron, American actor and evangelical Christian pro-creationism activist
  - Charlie Ward, American retired football and basketball player
- October 14 – Daniela Peštová, Czech supermodel
- October 15 – Ginuwine, African-American singer
- October 16 – Mehmet Scholl, German footballer
- October 17
  - Anil Kumble, Indian cricketer
  - Marciano Vink, Dutch footballer
- October 18 – Jose Padilla, American gang member and convicted terrorist
- October 20 – Michelle Malkin, American political commentator
- October 21
  - Louis Koo, Hong Kong actor
  - Tony Mortimer, English singer (East 17)
- October 24 – Raúl Esparza, American actor
- October 25 – Adam Goldberg, American actor
- October 27 – Adrian Erlandsson, Swedish drummer
- October 29
  - Phillip Cocu, Dutch footballer
  - Edwin van der Sar, Dutch footballer
- October 30
  - Ben Bailey, American host (*Cash Cab*)
  - Xie Jun, Chinese chess grandmaster

- Nia Long, African-American actress
- October 31 – Linn Berggren, Swedish singer (Ace of Base)

November

Ethan Hawke

Morgan Spurlock

- November 2
  - Ely Buendia, Filipino rock lead singer and rhythm guitarist (Eraserheads)
  - Sharmell Sullivan-Huffman, American World Wrestling Entertainment (WWE) valet and former Nitro Girl
- November 3 – Dawn Marie Psaltis, American Extreme Championship Wrestling (ECW) and WWE performer
- November 4 – Tony Sly, American punk rock lead vocalist (No Use for a Name) (d. 2012)

- November 5 – Javy López, American baseball player
- November 6 – Ethan Hawke, American actor, writer, and film director
- November 7
  - Morgan Spurlock, American filmmaker and activist (*Super-size Me*)
  - Neil Hannon, Northern Irish musician, The Divine Comedy
- November 8 – Tom Anderson, American co-founder of Myspace
- November 9
  - Chris Jericho, Canadian pro wrestler
  - Scarface, member of the rap group Geto Boys
- November 10 – Orny Adams, American comedian
- November 12 – Tonya Harding, American figure skater
- November 15
  - Patrick M'Boma, Cameroonian footballer
  - Jack Ingram, American country music singer
- November 16 – Martha Plimpton, American actress
- November 17
  - Paul Allender, English guitarist (Cradle of Filth)
  - Tania Zaetta, Australian actress and television presenter
- November 18 – Peta Wilson, Australian actress
- November 20 – Joe Zaso, American actor and producer
- November 21 – Karen Davila, Filipina broadcast journalist, TV host and news personality
- November 22 – Stel Pavlou, British novelist and screenwriter
- November 23
  - Zoë Ball, British television and radio presenter

- o Oded Fehr, Israeli-American actor
- November 26 – Dave Hughes, Australian comedian
- November 27
  - o Mr. Lobo, television personality/horror host
  - o Humberto Ramos, Mexican comic book penciller
- November 30
  - o Walter Emanuel Jones, American actor
  - o Natalie Williams, American basketball player

December

Sarah Silverman

Jennifer Connelly

Ted Cruz

- December 1 – Sarah Silverman, American comedian
- December 2 – Joshua Seth, American voice actor and hypnotist
- December 3 – Jimmy Shergill, Indian actor
- December 4 – Kevin Sussman, American actor
- December 5 – Tim Hetherington, English-born photojournalist (d. 2011)
- December 6 – Ulf "Buddha" Ekberg, Swedish rock musician (Ace of Base)
- December 9 – Kara DioGuardi, American songwriter
- December 12
  - Jennifer Connelly, American actress
  - Regina Hall, American actress
- December 15 – Michael Shanks, Canadian actor
- December 17 – Craig Doyle, Irish television presenter
- December 18
  - DMX, African-American rapper and actor
  - Miles Marshall Lewis, American author
  - Rob Van Dam, American pro wrestler
- December 20
  - Nicole de Boer, Canadian actress

- Massimo Ellul, Maltese entrepreneur and philanthropist
- December 22
  - Ted Cruz, Canadian-born American politician and junior United States Senator from Texas
  - Gary Anderson, Scottish darts player
  - Clay Dreslough, American game designer
- December 23 – Catriona Le May Doan, Canadian speed skater
- December 25 – Emmanuel Amuneke, Nigerian footballer
- December 29
  - Aled Jones, Welsh singer and television presenter
  - Kevin Weisman, American actor
- December 31 – Bryon Russell, American basketball player

Date unknown

- Przemysław Truściński, Polish artist

Deaths

January

Max Born

Bertrand Russell

- January 1 – Alfred Lauck Parson, British chemist and physicist (b. 1889)
- January 4
    - Jean-Étienne Valluy, French general (b. 1899)
    - David John Williams, Welsh-language writer and Welsh nationalist (b. 1885)
- January 5 – Max Born, German physicist, Nobel Prize laureate (b. 1882)

- January 7 – Robert Barrat, American actor (b. 1889)
- January 10 – Pavel Belyayev, Soviet cosmonaut (b. 1925)
- January 14 – Harry M. Woods, American songwriter (b. 1896)
- January 18 – David O. McKay, 9th president of The Church of Jesus Christ of Latter-day Saints (b. 1873)
- January 19 – Hal March, American actor (b. 1920)
- January 25
  - Jane Bathori, French mezzo-soprano (b. 1877)
  - Eiji Tsuburaya, Japanese film director and special effects designer (*Godzilla, Ultraman*) (b. 1901)
- January 27 – Rita Angus, New Zealand painter (b. 1908)
- January 28 – Thomas J. Ryan, American admiral (b. 1901)
- January 29
  - Lawren Harris, Canadian painter. (b. 1885)
  - Basil Liddell Hart, British military historian (b. 1895)
  - Thelma Morgan, American socialite (b. 1904)
- January 30 – Fritz Bayerlein, German general (b. 1899)
- January 31 – Slim Harpo, American singer (b. 1924)

February

- February 2
  - Lawrence Gray, American actor (b. 1898)
  - Bertrand Russell, English logician and philosopher, recipient of the Nobel Prize in Literature (b. 1872)
- February 3 – Italo Gariboldi, Italian general (b. 1879)
- February 4 – Louise Bogan, American poet (b. 1897)
- February 5 – Rudy York, American baseball player (b. 1913)
- February 6 – Roscoe Karns, American actor (b. 1891)

- February 10
  - John Davidson, Scottish-Canadian botanist. (b. 1878)
  - Tobias Geffen, Lithuanian-born, American American Orthodox rabbi who served the Congregation Shearith Israel in Atlanta, Georgia (1910–1970). He was also noted for certifying with Coca-Cola making the soft drink kosher. (b.1870)
  - Alfred Roberts, English lay preacher, politician, and father of Prime Minister of the United Kingdom (b. 1892)
- February 14
  - Arthur Edeson, American cinematographer (b. 1891)
  - Sasha Siemel, adventurer, hunter, guide, actor, writer, photographer, and lecturer. (b. 1890)
  - Harry Stradling, American cinematographer (b. 1901)
  - Herbert Strudwick, English cricketer (b. 1880)

  - Air Chief Marshal Hugh Dowding

- February 15 – Hugh Dowding, British RAF Fighter Commander during the Battle of Britain (b. 1882)
- February 16 – Francis Peyton Rous, American pathologist, recipient of the Nobel Prize in Physiology or Medicine (b. 1879)
- February 17
  - Shmuel Yosef Agnon, Israeli writer, Nobel Prize laureate (b. 1888)
  - Alfred Newman, American film composer (b. 1901)
- February 19 – Jules Munshin, American actor (b. 1915)
- February 20 – Sophie Treadwell, American playwright and journalist (b. 1885)
- February 21 – Johannes Semper, Estonian writer and translator (b. 1892)
- February 22 – Edward Selzer, American film producer (b. 1893)
- February 24 – Conrad Nagel, American actor (b. 1897)
- February 25
  - Mannathu Padmanabha Pillai, social reformer (b. 1878)
  - Mark Rothko, Latvian-born painter (b. 1903)
- February 26 – Terence Patrick O'Sullivan, engineer (b. 1913)

March

Heinrich Brüning

- March 6 – William Hopper, American actor (b. 1915)
- March 11
  - Erle Stanley Gardner, American crime writer(b. 1889)
  - Lucille Hegamin, American singer and entertainer (b. 1894)
- March 8 – Waldo Peirce, American painter (b. 1884)
- March 9 – Nicholas Timasheff, Russian sociologist (b. 1886)
- March 13 – Alec Clunes, English actor (b. 1912)
- March 14 – Ma Hongkui, prominent warlord in China during the Republic of China era (b. 1892)
- March 16 – Tammi Terrell, African-American singer (b. 1945)
- March 18 – William Beaudine, American film director (b. 1892)
- March 23 – Del Lord, Canadian film director (b. 1894)
- March 26 – Patricia Ellis, American actress (b. 1916)
- March 29 – Vera Brittain, British writer (b. 1893)
- March 30 – Heinrich Brüning, Chancellor of Germany (b. 1885)
- March 31
  - Semyon Timoshenko, Soviet general, Marshal of the Soviet Union (b. 1895)
  - George Wootten, Australian soldier, public servant, political activist and solicitor (b. 1893)

April

- April 5 – Alfred Henry Sturtevant, American geneticist (b. 1891)
- April 6 – Maurice Stokes, American basketball player (b. 1933)

- April 11
  - Cathy O'Donnell, American actress (b. 1923)
  - John O'Hara, American writer (b. 1905)
  - Joseph Schechtman, writer and Revisionist political activist (b. 1891)
- April 16 – Richard Neutra, Austrian American architect (b. 1892)
- April 23 – Herb Shriner, American humorist (b. 1918)
- April 25 – Anita Louise, American actress (b. 1915)
- April 26 – Gypsy Rose Lee, American actress (b. 1911)
- April 27 – Arthur Shields, Irish actor (b. 1896)
- April 28 – Ed Begley, American actor (b. 1901)
- April 30 – Inger Stevens, Swedish-born actress (b. 1934)

May

Nelly Sachs

- May 1
  - Yi Un, Crown Prince of Korea (b. 1897)
  - Ralph Hartley, American inventor (b. 1888)

- May 6
  - Giovanni Giuriati, Italian Fascist politician (b. 1876)
  - Helen Kinnear, Canadian lawyer (b. 1894)
- May 9
  - Andrew Watson Myles, Canadian politician (b. 1884)
  - Walter Reuther, American labor union leader (b. 1907)
- May 10
  - Mari Blanchard, American actress (b. 1927)
  - Leslie H. Sabo, Jr., Medal of Honor recipient (b. 1948)
- May 11 – Johnny Hodges, American jazz musician (b. 1906)
- May 12
  - Władysław Anders, General of the Polish Army (b. 1892)
  - Nelly Sachs, German writer, Nobel Prize laureate (b. 1891)
- May 13 – Sir William Dobell, Australian artist (b. 1899)
- May 14 – Billie Burke, American actress (b. 1885)
- May 17 – Heinz Hartmann, Austrian psychiatrist and psychoanalyst (b. 1894)
- May 19 – Ray Schalk, American baseball player (Chicago White Sox) and a member of the MLB Hall of Fame (b. 1892)
- May 21 – E. L. Grant Watson, Australian scientist and writer (b. 1885)
- May 22 – Joseph Wood Krutch, American writer and naturalist. (b. 1893)
- May 29
  - John Gunther, American writer (b. 1901)
  - Eva Hesse, German-born American sculptor (b. 1936)
- May 31 – Terry Sawchuk, Canadian hockey player (b. 1929)

June

Alexander Kerensky

Sukarno

- June 1 – George Watkins, American baseball player (b. 1900)
- June 2
    - Albert Lamorisse, French filmmaker (b. 1922)
    - Bruce McLaren, Formula 1 driver (b. 1937)
- June 3
    - Ruth Sawyer, American storyteller and writer (b. 1880)
    - Hjalmar Schacht, Nazi German economic minister (b. 1877)
- June 4 – Sonny Tufts, American actor (b. 1911)

- June 7 – E. M. Forster, English writer (b. 1879)
- June 8 – Abraham Maslow, American psychologist (b. 1908)
- June 11
  - Alexander Kerensky, Russian revolutionary politician (b. 1881)
  - Frank Laubach, working at a remote location in the Philippines (b. 1884)
- June 13 – Gonzalo Roig, Cuban musician, composer, musical director and founder of several orchestras.(b. 1890)
- June 14 – William H. Daniels, American cinematographer (b. 1901)
- June 15 – John Noble Kennedy, British Army officer (b. 1893)
- June 16
  - Heino Eller, Estonian composer and composition teacher (b. 1887)
  - Brian Piccolo, American football star (b. 1943)
- June 21 – Sukarno, President of Indonesia (b. 1901)
- June 22 – Frank J. Wilson, Chief of the United States Secret Service (b. 1887)
- June 26 – Leopoldo Marechal, Argentine writer (b. 1900)
- June 27 – Daniel Kinsey, American hurdler (b. 1902)
- June 30 – Arthur Leslie, British actor (b. 1901)

July

António de Oliveira Salazar

- July 6 – Marjorie Rambeau, American actress (b. 1889)
- July 10 – Bjarni Benediktsson, Icelandic foreign and later prime minister (b. 1908)
- July 12 – L. Wolfe Gilbert, Russian-born American songwriter. (b. 1886)
- July 11 – André Lurçat, French modernist architect, landscape architect, (b. 1894)
- July 14 – Preston Foster, American actor (b. 1900)
- July 15 – Frits Lugt, self-taught collector and connoisseur of Dutch drawings and prints and a selfless (b. 1884)
- July 17 – Ernst Wellmann, highly decorated German Army officer (b. 1904)
- July 19 – Egon Eiermann, German architect (b. 1904)
- July 21 – Bob Kalsu, American football player (b. 1945)
- July 22 – Fritz Kortner, Austrian-born director (b. 1892)
- July 24 – Peter de Noronha, Indian businessman (b. 1897)
- July 27 – António de Oliveira Salazar, Prime Minister of Portugal (de facto dictator) (b. 1889)
- July 28 – Baba Bujha Singh, Indian revolutionary

- July 29
  - John Barbirolli, English conductor (b. 1899)
  - George Szell, Hungarian conductor (b. 1897)
- July 31 – Wilfrid Kent Hughes, Australian Olympian and politician (b. 1895)

August

- August 1
  - Delia Akeley, American explorer. (b. 1875)
  - Frances Farmer, American actress (b. 1913)
  - Doris Fleeson, American journalist (b. 1901)
  - Otto Heinrich Warburg, German physician and physiologist, Nobel Prize in Physiology or Medicine laureate (b. 1883)
- August 18 – Soledad Miranda, Spanish actress (b. 1943)
- August 19 – Paweł Jasienica, Polish historian (b. 1909)
- August 20 – Mickey Daniels, American actor (b. 1914)
- August 22 – Vladimir Propp, Soviet folklorist (b. 1895)
- August 30
  - Thomas Hunton, Royal Marines officer (b. 1885)
  - William McCance, Scottish artist (b. 1894)

September

Jimi Hendrix

Gamal Abdel Nasser

- September 1 – François Mauriac, French writer, Nobel Prize laureate (b. 1885)
- September 2 – Marie-Pierre Koenig, French general and politician (b. 1898)
- September 3
  - Vince Lombardi, American football coach (b. 1913)
  - Alan Wilson, American blues rock musician (b. 1943)
- September 5
  - Jesse Pennington, English footballer (b. 1883)

- ○ Jochen Rindt, Austrian race car driver (b. 1942)
- September 7 – Yitzhak Gruenbaum, noted leader of the Zionist (b. 1879)
- September 11
  - ○ Ernst May, German architect (b. 1886)
  - ○ Chester Morris, American actor (b. 1901)
  - ○ Boes Boestami, Indonesian actor (b. 1922)
- September 18 – James Marshall "Jimi" Hendrix, American rock musician (b. 1942)
- September 22 – Alice Hamilton, the first woman appointed to the faculty of Harvard University (b. 1869)
- September 23 – André Bourvil, French actor (b. 1917)
- September 25 – Erich Maria Remarque, German author (*All Quiet On The Western Front*) (b. 1898)
- September 28
  - ○ John Dos Passos, American novelist (b. 1896)
  - ○ Gamal Abdel Nasser, second President of Egypt (b. 1918)
- September 29 – Edward Everett Horton, American actor (b. 1886)

October

Janis Joplin

- October 4 – Janis Joplin, American rock singer (*Mercedes Benz*) (b. 1943)
- October 10 – Édouard Daladier, French prime minister, signed Munich Agreement (b. 1884)
- October 13 – Julia Culp, mezzo-soprano (b. 1880)
- October 17 – Pierre Laporte, Canadian statesman (assassinated) (b. 1921)
- October 21
  - Ernest Haller, American cinematographer (b. 1896)
  - John T. Scopes, American Scopes Monkey Trial defendant (b. 1900)
- October 24 – Richard Hofstadter, American historian (b. 1916)
- October 25 – Ülo Sooster, Estonian painter (b. 1924)
- October 25 – Prince Felix of Bourbon-Parma,(b. 1893)

November

Charles de Gaulle

Chandrasekhara Venkata Raman

- November 2
  - Abram Samoilovitch Besicovitch, Russian mathematician (b. 1891)
  - Fernand Gravey, French actor (b. 1904)
- November 3 – Peter II of Yugoslavia, Last King of Yugoslavia (b. 1923)
- November 7 – Eddie Peabody, American musician (b. 1902)
- November 8 – Napoleon Hill, American author in the area of the new thought (b. 1883)
- November 9 – Charles de Gaulle, President of France (b. 1890)
- November 14
  - Louis Rich, American entrepreneur (b. 1896)
  - Howard Waldemar Winkler, Canadian politician (b. 1891)
- November 19 – Andrei Yeremenko, Soviet military leader, Marshal of the Soviet Union (b. 1892)
- November 20 – John Louis Clarke, Blackfoot wood carver from Montana. (b. 1881)
- November 21 – C. V. Raman, Indian physicist. (b. 1888)

- November 23 – Yusof bin Ishak, first President of Singapore (b. 1910)
- November 25
  - Louise Glaum, American actress (b. 1888)
  - Yukio Mishima, Japanese novelist (b. 1925)
- November 26 – David Brown (footballer, born 1887), Scottish footballer (b. 1887)
- November 27 – Helene Madison, American Olympic swimmer (b. 1913)
- November 29 – Robert T. Frederick, American combat commander (b. 1907)

December

- December 7 – Rube Goldberg, American cartoonist (b. 1883)
- December 8
  - Christopher Kelk Ingold, British chemist (b. 1893)
  - Philip Edward Smith, American endocrinologist (b. 1884)
- December 12 – Doris Blackburn, Australian politician (b. 1889)
- December 15 – Ernest Marsden, English-New Zealand physicist.(b. 1889)
- December 23 – Charles Ruggles, American actor (b. 1886)
- December 24 – Charles M. Cooke, Jr., American admiral (b. 1886)
- December 29 – Prince Adalbert of Bavaria (1886–1970) (b. 1886)
- December 30 – Lenore Ulric, American actress (b. 1892)
- December 31

- Ray Henderson, American songwriter (b. 1896)
- Cyril Scott, English composer, writer, and poet (b. 1879)

Nobel Prizes

- Physics – Hannes Alfvén, Louis Néel
- Chemistry – Luis Federico Leloir
- Medicine – Sir Bernard Katz, Ulf von Euler, Julius Axelrod
- Literature – Aleksandr Isaevich Solzhenitsyn
- Peace – Norman E. Borlaug
- Nobel Memorial Prize in Economic Sciences – Paul Samuelson

In the News.

1970 Music continues to make significant impact with the largest ever rock festival held on the Isle of Wight with 600,000 people.

Paul McCartney announces that the Beatles have disbanded.

Boeing 747 makes its first commercial passenger trip to London.

U.S Invades Cambodia.

100,000 people demonstrate in Washington DC against the Vietnam War.

Edward Heath and the Conservative Party wins the British general elections.

Brazil wins their third world cup with Pele as the captain.

Jimi Hendrix dies of barbiturate overdose in London.

Janis Joplin dies in a cheap motel from a heroin overdose.

The first New York marathon is run in New York.

The First Computer Chess Tournament takes Place.

1970 Calender.

January 1970

Sun	Mon	Tue	Wed	Thu	Fri	Sat
				1	2	3
4	5	6	7	8	9	10
11	12	13	14	15	16	17
18	19	20	21	22	23	24
25	26	27	28	29	30	31

February 1970

Sun	Mon	Tue	Wed	Thu	Fri	Sat
1	2	3	4	5	6	7
8	9	10	11	12	13	14
15	16	17	18	19	20	21
22	23	24	25	26	27	28

March 1970

Sun	Mon	Tue	Wed	Thu	Fri	Sat
1	2	3	4	5	6	7
8	9	10	11	12	13	14
15	16	17	18	19	20	21
22	23	24	25	26	27	28
29	30	31				

April 1970

Sun	Mon	Tue	Wed	Thu	Fri	Sat
			1	2	3	4
5	6	7	8	9	10	11
12	13	14	15	16	17	18
19	20	21	22	23	24	25
26	27	28	29	30		

May 1970

Sun	Mon	Tue	Wed	Thu	Fri	Sat
					1	2
3	4	5	6	7	8	9
10	11	12	13	14	15	16
17	18	19	20	21	22	23
24	25	26	27	28	29	30
31						

June 1970

Sun	Mon	Tue	Wed	Thu	Fri	Sat
	1	2	3	4	5	6
7	8	9	10	11	12	13
14	15	16	17	18	19	20
21	22	23	24	25	26	27
28	29	30				

July 1970

Sun	Mon	Tue	Wed	Thu	Fri	Sat
			1	2	3	4
5	6	7	8	9	10	11
12	13	14	15	16	17	18
19	20	21	22	23	24	25
26	27	28	29	30	31	

August 1970

Sun	Mon	Tue	Wed	Thu	Fri	Sat
						1
2	3	4	5	6	7	8
9	10	11	12	13	14	15
16	17	18	19	20	21	22
23	24	25	26	27	28	29
30	31					

September 1970

Sun	Mon	Tue	Wed	Thu	Fri	Sat
		1	2	3	4	5
6	7	8	9	10	11	12
13	14	15	16	17	18	19
20	21	22	23	24	25	26
27	28	29	30			

October 1970

Sun	Mon	Tue	Wed	Thu	Fri	Sat
				1	2	3
4	5	6	7	8	9	10
11	12	13	14	15	16	17
18	19	20	21	22	23	24
25	26	27	28	29	30	31

November 1970

Sun	Mon	Tue	Wed	Thu	Fri	Sat
1	2	3	4	5	6	7
8	9	10	11	12	13	14
15	16	17	18	19	20	21
22	23	24	25	26	27	28
29	30					

December 1970

Sun	Mon	Tue	Wed	Thu	Fri	Sat
		1	2	3	4	5
6	7	8	9	10	11	12
13	14	15	16	17	18	19
20	21	22	23	24	25	26
27	28	29	30	31		

www.ingramcontent.com/pod-product-compliance
Lightning Source LLC
Chambersburg PA
CBHW071230280526
45787CB00002B/863